# two treasures

Other Parallax Press Books
by Thich Nhat Hanh

*Being Peace*

*Call Me by My True Names:*
*The Collected Poems of Thich Nhat Hanh*

*Calming the Fearful Mind:*
*A Zen Response to Terrorism*

*The Energy of Prayer:*
*How to Deepen Your Spiritual Practice*

*Keeping the Peace:*
*Mindfulness and Public Service*

*Old Path White Clouds*

*Present Moment Wonderful Moment*

*Teachings on Love*

*Touching Peace*

*Understanding Our Mind*

# thich nhat hanh

## two treasures

*Buddhist Teachings on Awakening
and True Happiness*

Parallax Press
Berkeley, CA

Parallax Press
P.O. Box 7355
Berkeley, California 94707
www.parallax.org

Parallax Press is the publishing division of Unified Buddhist
Church, Inc.

Edited by Rachel Neumann.
Cover and text design by Debbie Berne, Herter Studio LLC

Library of Congress Cataloging-in-Publication Data

Nhat Hanh, Thich.
  Two treasures : Buddhist teachings on awakening and true happiness / Thich Nhat Hanh.
    p. cm.
  Includes bibliographical references.
  ISBN 1-888375-68-X (mini pbk.)
  1. Ba da ren jue jing–Commentaries. 2. Tipitaka. Suttapitaka. Khuddakanikaya. Khuddakapatha Mangalasutta–Commentaries. I. Ba
da ren jue jing. English. II. Tipitaka. Suttapitaka. Khuddakanikaya.
Khuddakapatha. Mangalasutta. English. III. Title.
  BQ1529.5.P347N53 2007
  294.3'8232–dc22

                                        2006028066

1 2 3 4 5 / 11 10 09 08 07

# table *of* contents

WHEN I WAS SEVENTEEN and in my first year of novice studies at a Buddhist monastery in Vietnam, I had to memorize the Sutra on the Eight Realizations of the Great Beings and the Discourse on Happiness. Over sixty years have passed, and I still find these two texts to be torches that help light my path.

In 1978, I became involved in a project to rescue Vietnamese boat people in the South China Sea. We printed the Sutra on the Eight Realizations of the Great Beings in a small booklet in Vietnamese to help the

survivors as they found a new home some-
where in the world. Soon, we found this sutra, as well as the Discourse on Happiness, to
be very helpful for those in the West as well.
All of us, whatever our past experiences, are
struggling to find happiness and realize full
consciousness in our daily lives.

I invite you to read this book at a time
when your body and mind are completely
relaxed, for example after taking a comfort-
able bath. You can light a candle or a stick
of incense to give the room a pleasant glow
or fragrance. Then, read one of these sutras
slowly to discover its deepest meaning. These
sutras are thousands of years old, but it is
only by relating them to your own life's experience that they come alive and you can
understand them.

The more you meditate on these sutras,
the more deeply you will discover the pro-

found wisdom they contain. The two sutras in this book complement each other. They can be read separately, but together they explain in practical detail how to progress step-by-step toward awakening and happiness.

*Thich Nhat Hanh*
*July, 2006*

*the sutra on the*
*eight realizations*
*of the great beings*[1]


WHOLEHEARTEDLY, day and night, a disciple
of the Buddha should recite and meditate on
the eight realizations discovered by the great
beings.

The First Realization is the awareness
that the world is impermanent. All political
regimes are subject to fall; all things composed of the four elements are empty and
contain the seeds of suffering.[2] Human beings are composed of five *skandha* (aggregates) and are without a separate self.[3] They
are always in the process of change—con-

stantly being born and constantly dying.
They are empty of self, without sovereignty.
The mind is the source of all confusion, and
the body is the forest of all impure actions. If
we meditate on these facts, we can gradually
be released from *samsara*, the round of birth
and death.

The Second Realization is the awareness that more desire brings more suffering.
All hardships in daily life arise from greed
and desire. Those with little desire and ambi-
tion are able to relax, their bodies and minds
free from entanglement.

The Third Realization is that the human mind is always searching for possessions
and never feels fulfilled. This causes impure
actions to ever increase. Bodhisattvas however, always remember the principle of having
few desires.[4] They live a simple life in peace
in order to practice the Way, and consider

the realization of perfect understanding as their only career.

The Fourth Realization is the awareness of the extent to which laziness is an obstacle to practice. For this reason, we must practice diligently to destroy the unwholesome mental factors that bind us, and to conquer the four kinds of Mara,[5] in order to free ourselves from the prisons of the five aggregates and the three worlds.[6]

The Fifth Realization is the awareness that ignorance is the cause of the endless round of birth and death. Therefore, bodhisattvas always remember to listen and learn in order to develop their understanding and eloquence. This enables them to educate living beings and bring them to the realm of great joy.

The Sixth Realization is the awareness that poverty creates hatred and anger, which creates a vicious cycle of negative thoughts and activity. When practicing generosity, bodhisattvas consider everyone, friends and enemies alike, as equal. They do not condemn anyone's past wrongdoings, nor do they hate those who are presently causing harm.

The Seventh Realization is that the five categories of desire lead to difficulties.[7] Although we are in the world, we should try not to be caught up in worldly matters. A monk, for example, has in his possession only three robes and one bowl. He lives simply in order to practice the Way. His precepts keep him free of attachment to worldly things, and he treats everyone equally and with compassion.

The Eighth Realization is the awareness that the fire of birth and death is raging, causing endless suffering everywhere. We should take the Great Vow to help everyone,

*the sutra on the eight realizations*

to suffer with everyone, and to guide all beings to the realm of great joy.

These eight realizations are the discoveries of great beings, buddhas, and bodhisattvas who have diligently practiced the way of compassion and understanding. They have sailed the *Dharmakaya*[8] boat to the shore of nirvana, but then they return to the ordinary world, having abandoned the five desires, with their minds and hearts directed toward the noble way, using these eight realizations to help all beings recognize the suffering in this world.[9] If the disciples of the Buddha recite these eight realizations and meditate on them, they will put an end to countless misunderstandings and difficulties and progress toward enlightenment, leaving behind the world of birth and death, dwelling forever in peace.

*commentary on*
*the sutra on the*
*eight realizations*
*of the great beings*

THE MOST ACCESSIBLE WAY to approach the Sutra on the Eight Realizations of the Great Beings is to see each of the eight items discussed as a subject of meditation. In addition, there are eleven guidelines for daily living that can be found in the sutra. Although the form of the sutra is simple, its content is extremely profound and marvelous. This sutra is not an analytical treatise or a historical artifact; it's a realistic and effective approach to meditation and a guide for our interactions with others.

### THE FIRST REALIZATION

The first realization explains and clarifies the four basic subjects of Buddhist meditation: impermanence, suffering, no-self, and impurity. We must always remember and meditate on these four principles of reality. As mentioned in the sutra, if someone meditates on these facts, she will gradually be released from samsara, the round of birth and death.

*Impermanence*

This refers to the transient nature of all things. From moment to moment, all things in this world, including human life, mountains, rivers, political systems, are in constant transformation. This is called impermanence in each moment. Everything passes through a period of birth, maturity, transformation, and destruction. This destruction is called impermanence in each cycle. To see the impermanent nature of all things, we must examine this closely. Doing so will prevent us from being imprisoned by the things of this world.

## Suffering

Suffering has to do with the emptiness of all things. The ancient people of India said that all things are composed of four elements: earth, air, water, and fire. Acknowledging this, buddhas and bodhisattvas understand that when there is a harmonious relationship among the four elements, there is peace. When the four elements are not in harmony, there is suffering.

Because all things are created by a combination of these elements, nothing can exist independently or permanently. All things are impermanent. Consequently, when we are caught up in the things of the world, we suffer from their impermanent nature. And since all things are empty, when we are caught by things, we also suffer from their emptiness. Awareness of the existence of suffering leads us to begin to practice the way of realization. This is the first of the Four Noble Truths.[10] When we lose awareness of and do not meditate on the existence of suffering in all things, we can easily be pushed around by passions and desires for worldly things, increasingly destroying our lives in the pursuit of these desires. Only by being aware of suffering can we find its cause, confront it directly, and eliminate it.

## Selflessness (no-self)

Buddhism teaches that human beings are composed of five aggregates, called skandhas in Sanskrit. If the form created by the four elements is empty and without self, then human beings, created by the unification of the five skandhas, must also be empty and without self. Human beings are involved in a transformation process from second to second, minute to minute, continually experiencing impermanence in each moment. By looking very deeply into the five skandhas, we can experience the selfless nature of our bodies, our passage through birth and death, and emptiness, thereby destroying the illusion that our bodies are permanent. In Buddhism, no-self is the most important subject for meditation. By meditating on no-self, we can break through the barrier between self and other. When we no longer are separate from the universe, a completely harmonious existence with the universe is created. We see that all other human beings exist in us and that we exist in all other human beings. We see that the past and the future are contained in the present moment, and we can penetrate and be completely liberated from the cycle of birth and death.

Modern science has also discovered the truth of the selfless nature of all things. The approach of British biologist Lyall Watson, for example, corresponds entirely with the principle of dependent origination and no-self.[11] Scientists who meditate continuously on the selfless nature of their own bodies and minds, as well as the selfless nature of all things, will one day easily attain enlightenment.

*Impurity*

In terms of the nature of our bodies and minds, impurity means the absence of an immaculate state of being, one that is neither holy nor beautiful. From the Buddhist psychological and physiological standpoint, all human beings are impure. This is not a negative judgment, but an objective perspective on human beings. If we examine the constituents of our bodies from the hair on our head to the blood, pus, phlegm, excrement, urine, the many bacteria dwelling in the intestines, and the many diseases present waiting for the opportunity to develop, it seems clear that our bodies are impure and subject to decay. Our bodies also create the motivation to pursue the satisfaction of our desires and passions. That is why the sutra regards the body as the place where misdeeds gather.

Similarly, the mind is the place where misunderstandings gather. Since we are unable to see the truth of impermanence, suffering, and the selfless nature of all things, our minds often become the victims of greed

and hatred, and we act as if we are individ-
ual isolated beings who will live forever. So
the sutra says, "The mind is the source of all
confusion."

## THE SECOND REALIZATION

"More desire brings more suffering" is the
basis of the second realization. Most people
define happiness as the satisfaction of all desires. There are five types of desire.[12] These
desires are boundless but our ability to realize them is not, and unfulfilled desires always
create suffering. When desires are only par-
tially fulfilled, we continue to pursue their
complete fulfillment, and we create more
suffering. Even when a desire is fulfilled, we
suffer when its fulfillment terminates. It is
only after we become completely exhausted
from this incessant pursuit that we begin to

realize the extent to which we were caught in the insatiable net of desires and passions. Then we can realize that true happiness is really a peaceful state of body and mind, and this can only exist when our desires are few. Having few desires and not seeking fulfillment through the pursuit of the five desires are great steps toward liberation.

### THE THIRD REALIZATION

Knowing how to feel satisfied with few possessions destroys desire and greed. This means being content with material conditions that allow us to be healthy and strong enough to practice the Way. This is an effective way to cut through the net of passions and desires, attain a peaceful state of body and mind, have more time to help others, and be free to realize the highest goal: the development of concentration and understanding to attain realization. Knowing how to feel satisfied with few possessions helps us avoid buying unnecessarily and becoming part of an economic system that exploits others, and it enables us to decrease our involvement in the pollution of our environment.

### THE FOURTH REALIZATION

Diligent practice destroys laziness. After we cease looking for joy in desires and passions and know how to feel satisfied with few possessions, we must not be lazy, letting days and months slip by neglectfully. Great patience and diligence are needed continually to develop our concentration and understanding in the endeavor of self-realization. We must use all of our time to meditate on the four truths of impermanence, suffering,

selflessness, and impurity, the first four subjects of meditation. We must penetrate deeply into the profound meaning of The Four
Foundations of Mindfulness,[13] practicing,
studying, and meditating on the postures
and cycles (becoming, maturing, transformation, and destruction) of our bodies as
well as our feelings, sensations, mental formations, and consciousness. We should read
sutras and other writings that explain meditation, correct sitting, and controlling the
breath, such as the Satipatthana Sutta and
The Mahaprajñaparamita Heart Sutra. We
have to follow the teachings of these sutras
and practice them in an intelligent way,
choosing the methods that best apply to our
own situation. As necessary, we can modify
the methods suggested in order to accommo-
date our own needs. Our energy must also be
regulated until all the basic desires and pas-

sions—greed, anger, narrow-mindedness, arrogance, doubt, and preconceived ideas— are uprooted. At this time we will know that our bodies and minds are liberated from the imprisonment of birth and death, the five skandhas, and the three worlds.

### THE FIFTH REALIZATION

Concentration and understanding destroy narrow-mindedness. Among the basic desires and passions, narrow-mindedness has the deepest roots. When these roots are loosened, all other desires and passions—greed, anger, doubt, and preconceived ideas— are also uprooted. Knowing this, we can make a great effort to meditate on the truths of impermanence, no-self, and the dependent origination of all things. Once the roots of ignorance are severed, we can liberate ourselves and teach others to break through the chains of birth and death.

The first four subjects of meditation are to help us attain liberation. The next four subjects have the aim of helping others attain liberation, thus clearly and solidly uniting Theravada and Mahayana Buddhist thought.

## THE SIXTH REALIZATION

Every person, no matter what their wealth, is equally capable of practicing generosity. Some people think that they can practice generosity only if they are wealthy. This isn't true. Some people who are very wealthy do practice generosity, but many only do charity with the aim of gaining merit, profiting, or pleasing others. People whose lives are grounded in compassion are seldom rich because they share whatever they have with others. They are not willing to enrich their lives financially at the cost of others' poverty. Many people misunderstand the Buddhist expression "practicing generosity" to mean casually giving five or ten cents to a beggar on the street if we happen to have it in our pockets.

The practice of generosity is more beautiful than that. It is both modest and grand. Practicing generosity means continually acting in a way that will help equalize the difference between the wealthy and the impoverished. Whatever we do to ease human suffering and create social justice can be considered practicing generosity. That is not to say that we must become active in any political system. To engage in partisan political action that leads to a power struggle among opposing parties and causes death and destruction is not what we mean by practicing generosity.

How can a person practicing "knowing how to feel satisfied with few possessions" also practice generosity? It is by living simply. Almost everyone who spends his or her life serving and helping others, sacrificing themselves for the sake of humanity, lives simply. If they live their lives worrying about making money and gaining merit, how can they practice generosity? Mahatma Gandhi lived a very simple life; nevertheless his merit helping humanity and saving human beings was immeasurable. There are thousands of people among us who live very simply, while being very helpful to many, many others. They do not have as great a reputation as Gandhi, but their merit is no less than his. It is enough for us just to be a little more attentive and aware of the presence of people like these. They do not practice generosity by giving money that they do not possess, but rather by giving their time, energy, love, and care—their entire lives.

Practicing generosity in a Buddhist context means to consider everyone equal, not to discriminate against anyone. There are cruel persons and kind persons among the poor and destitute, just as there are among the wealthy, and we must not exclude the cruel ones from our practice.

As the sutra states, "Bodhisattvas consider everyone, friends and enemies alike, as equal. They do not condemn anyone's past wrongdoings, nor do they hate those who are presently doing harm." This expresses the spirit of Mahayana Buddhism. Poverty creates anger, hatred, and wrongdoing. If we teach Buddhist philosophy though lectures, but do not practice generosity to ease the suffering of others, we have not yet attained the essence of Buddhism. We should practice generosity with compassion and not disdain, without discriminating against people who, because of their poverty, have caused anger and hatred.

### THE SEVENTH REALIZATION

While living in society, we should not be defiled by it. We must live in harmony with society in order to help others, without being caught by the five desires, living like the lotus flower that blooms in the mud and yet remains pure and unstained. Practicing the way of liberation does not mean avoiding society, but helping in it. Before our capacity to help becomes strong and solid, we may be defiled by living in society. For this reason, bodhisattvas meditate on the detrimental nature of the five desires and firmly decide to live simply in order to practice generosity without discrimination. Thus, living in society and not being stained by it is to practice the *six paramitas*. Paramita means to help others reach the other shore, the shore of liberation from sickness, poverty, hunger, ignorance, desires and passions, and birth and death. The six paramitas are: giving, observing the precepts, using diligent effort, endurance, concentration, and understanding.

### THE EIGHTH REALIZATION

We should create in ourselves the firm decision to help others. We must make a deep and solemn vow to overcome the difficulties, dangers, and suffering that may occur while helping others. Since the suffering in society is limitless, the willingness and devotion to practice the way of helping others must also be limitless. Thus, the Mahayana spirit is an endless source of energy that inspires us to practice generosity without discrimination. With the Mahayana spirit, we can withstand the many challenges and humiliations encountered in society and are able to continue to practice the Way. This will bring great happiness to others.

## ELEVEN GUIDELINES
### FOR DAILY LIFE

The Mahayana Buddhist practice of the six paramitas is, in part, inspired by this sutra.

The Sutra on the Eight Realizations of the Great Beings is a great resource for meditation. But it is not intended for us to simply meditate on this sutra and then to continue living our lives as before. To fully benefit from this sutra, we must also practice and observe its teachings. Here are eleven guidelines for daily life, based on the insights found in the sutra:

### 1

While meditating on the body, do not hope or pray to be exempt from sickness. Without sickness, desires and passions can easily arise.

### 2

While acting in society, do not hope or pray not to have any difficulties. Without difficulties, arrogance can easily arise.

### 3

While meditating on the mind, do not hope or pray not to encounter hindrances. Without hindrances, present knowledge will not be challenged or broadened.

**4**

While working, do not hope or pray not to encounter obstacles. Without obstacles, the vow to help others will not deepen.

**5**

While developing a plan, do not hope or pray to achieve success easily. With easy success, arrogance can easily arise.

**6**

While interacting with others, do not hope or pray to gain personal profit. With the hope for personal gain, the spiritual nature of the encounter is diminished.

**7**

While speaking with others, do not hope or pray not to be disagreed with. Without disagreement, self-righteousness can flourish.

**8**

While helping others, do not hope or pray to be paid. With the hope of remuneration, the act of helping others will not be pure.

**9**

If you see personal profit in an action, do not participate in it. Even minimal participation will stir up desires and passions.

**10**

When wrongly accused, do not attempt to exonerate yourself. Attempting to defend yourself will create needless anger and animosity.

**11**

The Buddha spoke of sickness and suffering as effective medicines. Times of difficulties and accidents are also times of freedom and realization. Obstacles can be a form of liberation. The Buddha reminded us that the army of evil can be the guards of the Dharma. Difficulties are required for success. The person who mistreats one can be one's good friend. One's enemies are as an orchard or garden. The act of doing someone a favor can be as base as the act of casting away a pair of old shoes. The abandonment of material possessions can be wealth and being wrongly accused can be the source of strength to work for justice.

*the discourse on happiness*

I HEARD THESE WORDS of the Buddha one time when the Lord was living in the vicinity of Savatthi at the Anathapindika Monastery in the Jeta Grove. Late at night, a deva appeared whose light and beauty made the whole Jeta Grove shine radiantly. After paying respects to the Buddha, the deva asked him a question in the form of a verse:

"Many gods and men are eager to know
what are the greatest blessings
which bring about a peaceful and happy life.

Please, Tathagata, will you teach us?"

(This is the Buddha's answer):
"Not to be associated with the foolish ones,
To live in the company of wise people,
Honoring those who are worth honoring—
This is the greatest happiness.

"To live in a good environment,
To have planted good seeds
And to realize that you are on the right
path—
This is the greatest happiness.

"To have a chance to learn and grow,
To be skillful in your profession or craft,
Practicing the precepts and loving speech—
This is the greatest happiness.

"To be able to serve and support your
parents,
To cherish your own family,

To have a vocation that brings you joy—
This is the greatest happiness.

"To live honestly, generous in giving,
To offer support to relatives and friends,
Living a life of blameless conduct—
This is the greatest happiness.

"To avoid unwholesome actions,
Not caught by alcoholism or drugs,
And to be diligent in doing good things—
This is the greatest happiness.

"To be humble and polite in manner,
To be grateful and content with a simple
life,
Not missing the occasion to learn the
Dharma—
This is the greatest happiness.

"To persevere and be open to change,
To have regular contact with monks and nuns,

And to fully participate in Dharma discussions—
This is the greatest happiness.

"To live diligently and attentively,
To perceive the Noble Truths,
And to realize nirvana—
This is the greatest happiness.

"To live in the world
With your heart undisturbed by the world,
With all sorrows ended, dwelling in peace—
This is the greatest happiness.

"For the one who accomplishes this
Is unvanquished wherever she goes;
Always he is safe and happy—
Happiness lives within oneself."

*commentary on*
*the discourse on happiness*

THE PALI VERSION of this sutra is called the Mangala Sutta.[14] *Mangala* means a good omen, a forewarning of something to come, usually something positive that will bring happiness and prosperity. The word also connotes a blessing because in this sutra the Buddha teaches about the most important blessings, those things that bring happiness.

As with the Sutra on the Eight Realizations of the Great Beings, this sutra can be broken down, stanza by stanza, for meditation, as well as reflected on as a whole. For

ease, each stanza is repeated below, followed
by the related commentary.

*"Not to be associated with the foolish ones,*
*To live in the company of wise people,*
*Honoring those who are worth honoring—*
*This is the greatest happiness."*

The greatest blessing is to have good, wise,
kindhearted friends close by. We can't be
happy unless we have a sane, healthy space
within us and around us. We need a habitat
that is beautiful and nourishing, and that
gives us the safety and the freedom that we
need.

It is a great blessing to be among brothers, sisters, and friends who are practicing
kindness and refraining from violence, steal-
ing, and cruelty, and not caught up in addiction to alcohol, drugs, or gambling.

A community that practices love and understanding is the best antidote to addiction to drugs, alcohol, and casual and careless sex. When people suffer, they look for these distractions in order to forget their pain. But these things only distract us temporarily from our suffering, they don't heal us.

Our community can be a family that sustains us. We can't handpick everybody with whom we interact in our daily life, but we can chose to live among those who are kind and virtuous. When we can interact with those who are honorable and have great virtue, we are creating conditions that will bring us lasting happiness.

*"To live in a good environment,*
*To have planted good seeds*
*And to realize that you are on the right path—*
*This is the greatest happiness."*

"To live in a good environment," means to live in a place where the surroundings and all the activities have the purpose of nourishing us and building community. Without this base environment, we can't go very far. When we practice meditation together, eat together, or work together in a loving and aware way, we are nourishing our peace and harmony.

The physical environment and the presence of others is very important. Often, if we are home alone, even sitting for fifteen minutes of meditation seems impossible. We think we have so many other things to do, or perhaps we feel silly sitting alone like that. But if everyone around us is sitting, we find it much easier! That's why creating a nourishing environment is crucial. Only with this support, can we be a source of joy for ourselves and others.

commentary on the discourse

Community—called *Sangha* in Buddhism—and time are the two ingredients of the universal medicine. If you can take that medicine every day for a number of years, then you have a chance. You become a plant, a tree, deeply rooted in the soil of the Sangha. Happiness and love become possible. And then you can go back and help your own blood family, your own spiritual community, and your society.

It's crucial that we all learn the art of Sangha building and figure out how to create a nourishing, harmonious environment in our lifetime. If we do not have this base, then there is nothing to keep us on the right path and keep us from entering the hell realms or the realm of the hungry ghosts. We don't need to leave this Earth to look for hell. Hell realms are everywhere, even in the town in which we live. There are hell realms that we have visited, or that we have lived through, and we know that these hell realms are real. We may have been caught in situations of abuse, violence, cruelty, fear, or addiction. We may have been carried away by strong emotions, such as hatred, jealousy, or infatuation, and so committed unwholesome actions. And we know that all over the world countless living beings are suffering in situations of war, poverty, injustice, and environmental destruction.

Hungry ghosts are demons who are perpetually craving food but are unable to take in nourishment. Hungry ghosts are not a myth—they live among us as people who may have enough food and clothing but who are still hungry for knowledge, for love, for hope, and for something to believe in. We have to build community a little bit everywhere so these hungry ghosts can find refuge. It is the atmosphere of harmony and community that can help the hungry ghosts get rooted and undo their knots of suffering.

With our nourishing community around us, we can find the right path to stability, ease, and liberation. Having a path is wonderful. Seeing the path is already great happiness. There is no reason to be fearful or confused anymore. Once we have recognized the path, our sense of loss, confusion, and despair dissipate. Happiness becomes immediately possible.

*"To have a chance to learn and grow,*
*To be skillful in your profession or craft,*
*Practicing the precepts and loving speech—*
*This is the greatest happiness."*

"To have a chance to learn and grow," means to have the opportunity to have a good education as well as to learn the Dharma. Learning is something that must happen every day, even for the Buddha! We want to have a vocation that does not cause harm to others or to the environment. When we can learn and practice our skills at the same time we support ourselves and our families, this is already a great blessing. There are many lucrative vocations that keep us twisting and turning in bed at night because they are not ethical. Those vocations cause harm to others or to the environment, and they force us to lie and hide the truth. Even though these jobs may be lucrative, they cause us a lot of suffering, suffering that goes deep into our soul. When we are able to find a job that expresses our ideal of compassion, happiness arises, even if the job is not as lucrative. Having a vocation that does not cause harm to others, to the environment, and through which we can express our compassion is a cause for great happiness.

Two thousand five hundred years ago, the Buddha offered his lay students five precepts or guidelines to help them live a peaceful, wholesome, and happy life. We call them the Five Mindfulness Trainings. Mindfulness—the awareness of what is going on in our body, our feelings, our mind, and in the world—is the basis of each training. With mindfulness, we can avoid harming ourselves and others, we protect ourself, our family, and our society, and we ensure safety and happiness now and in the future.

Even if we are happy in our work and following the precepts, it still requires daily commitment to practice loving speech and refrain from speaking to others with harsh words. When we use loving speech, we avoid misunderstanding and much suffering. Even if other people use harsh language when talking to us, we will suffer less if we use only loving speech in return. When we have understanding and compassion, we have lightness and we can communicate well with other people, even those who are violent and cruel. We can accept them; we know they are unhappy and that they are victims of their own anger, violence, and discrimination. When compassion and understanding are in us, we are no longer motivated by the desire for punishment or revenge. Loving speech becomes available to us and communication becomes possible.

Without real communication, happiness can't exist. To be surrounded by family, friends, and a spiritual community that know how to use loving speech is a great daily blessing. Because happiness is possible

here on Earth, the Buddha often spoke of
practical blessings such as this.

*"To be able to serve and support your parents,*
*To cherish your own family,*
*To have a vocation that brings you joy—*
*This is the greatest happiness."*

Your parents are the ones who raised you
and cared for you when you were little. Now
that you are an adult, you can support your
parents as they supported you. That is the
highest blessing. There are many ways to
support parents. We can offer financial support if we have that resource, but we can also
offer spiritual and emotional support. Financial offerings are wonderful; however, more
people suffer spiritually than financially.
If we know how to practice and keep the

mindfulness trainings, then we become a pillar of our family, able to support them in times of suffering and difficulty.

A long monastic history demonstrates this point. Although monastics don't hold jobs in the secular world and don't have money to send home to their parents, if they practice diligently, with equanimity and happiness, they are able to help many people and their family also benefits from this. In difficult times, they can be spiritual leaders, bringing reconciliation to their families.

A monk who practices successfully becomes the spiritual leader in his family, even though he may be very young. When a monastic opens her heart to intervene, her brothers, sisters, aunts, and uncles listen to her because she represents a source of spiritual love.

We do not need to become monastics

to have this role in our families. If we use loving speech, let go of our attachment to outcomes, and base our acts on compassion and love instead of anger and jealousy, we can become pillars of support for our families.

As a practitioner, our aim is not to make a lot of money. Our aim is to transform the suffering in our heart, to live in equanimity, peace, and happiness, and to offer happiness to our family and those around us. Our happiness multiplies exponentially when we see that we can bring happiness to those around us. This is reality, not superstition. In a retreat of five hundred people, there may be hundreds of them who come back to thank us after they have practiced. We can see the transformation in them. As each of us becomes more at ease and more aware of our capacity to love, we are more able to reconcile with our families and our loved ones if there has been conflict. Easing a long conflict with a loved one is a great source of happiness right in that very moment. We don't need to wait ten years to reap the happiness that is the fruit of our practice.

*"To live honestly, generous in giving,*
*To offer support to relatives and friends,*
*Living a life of blameless conduct—*
*This is the greatest happiness."*

"To live honestly" is to act virtuously, to be just, and to offer ourselves to life. To be generous is not simply to share our money, material resources, and technical knowledge; generosity does not require money. The offering of wealth, goods, or knowledge is only one of the many forms of generosity. There is a second form of generosity, offering the

Dharma. We can always offer and model the way to practice to alleviate suffering. This offering is much more precious than the financial offering. Most precious is the third kind of offering, the gift of non-fear, *abhaya*. The greatest gift in life is to live without fear and to teach others to do so as well. The offering of material goods, of the Dharma, and of non-fear are gifts from Avalokiteshvara Bodhisattva.

Many people are victims of their fear. If we can alleviate someone's fear, that is the greatest gift that we can offer them. Our life will be filled with happiness if we can help others around us. But if we spend our whole life building up our name and our fortune, then we cannot find happiness. We might have a lot of money, a big house, a luxurious car, but that's not real happiness. We can only taste real happiness when we can help others around us. And we have to start with those in our family and the dear friends around us. We have to help family, relatives, and friends first before we are capable of helping others outside our circle. If we're successful in helping our brothers and sisters in the Sangha, then we definitely will be able to help our loved ones. If, in our daily life, we can't help our brothers and sisters, then how can we offer help to others? We have to be successful in helping the people around us alleviate their suffering. That is the highest blessing, and that blessing has a lasting effect.

To be able to act without regret is a source of great happiness. This means we have nothing to regret in our words or actions toward others. We should be able to ask ourselves, "Have I done anything to my teacher, my friend, my father, my mother, that has made me feel regret later?" Asking this question will help us avoid any hint of regret, and will ensure that our speech and actions will not cause harm to others.

When our speech and actions cause no harm, we face a future without remorse. If we are burdened with regret, happiness is impossible. If we have erred in the past, or said something that caused harm, we can transform that past action and regret through the process of Beginning Anew.[15] We can commit ourselves to acting and speaking peacefully in the future, and then lasting happiness will again be available to us. If we can transform our mind and be determined not to say things or act in ways that will cause regret, then our mind will be cleansed and become luminous, and all the mistakes and errors of the past will completely disappear.

This is practicing according to the teaching of the Buddha. The errors originated in our mind, and when we transform our mind, we have the determination to refrain from committing the same errors in the future. When we transform our mind, we are immediately cleansed. The guilt we feel is lifted and the dark past disappears. This is called the practice of Beneficial Regret and Beginning Anew. Only when we're determined to make a vow to ourselves and our Sangha that we will not commit such acts or speak such words, can our error and our guilt be lifted. But this requires a strong determination and our determination won't be strong if we don't make this vow in front of both our Sangha and the Buddha.

Thus, kneeling down to prostrate, practicing Beginning Anew, and taking the Five Mindfulness Trainings with determination and resolve, will instantly make our guilt from the past disappear. When the mind is no longer loaded with guilt, then the guilt no longer exists. That's the principle of Beneficial Regret and Beginning Anew in Buddhism, being able to act without a hint of guilt. In English we can also call it "blameless conduct."

*"To avoid unwholesome actions,*
*Not caught by alcoholism or drugs,*
*And to be diligent in doing good things—*
*This is the greatest happiness."*

Our society is organized in such a way that it creates lonely people by the tens of thousands every day. And when we carry such despair and loneliness within us, it creates a vacuum. We feel compelled to fill that vacuum and forget our suffering with drugs, alcohol, careless sex, and the kind of entertainment that destroys our bodies and minds. Guns, armies, and prisons can't solve the problem of drugs and alcohol. The only way to ease this sense of emptiness and loneliness is to create an environment where young people can live joyfully. And if we ourselves don't live joyfully, we can't help our children or provide them with a good environment either.

Any speech, act, or thought that we feel might cause harm to others or to ourselves, is unwholesome. Even a joke that causes others to suffer or hurts their feelings is unwholesome. Not only do the victims suffer, but the perpetrators also share the suffering. Though others can't read your mind, you still suffer from negative thoughts. You may suffer tremendously, even if you're the only one who knows it.

Anything that clouds our mind is considered an intoxicant, whether it is drugs, alcohol, or gossip. We consume these intoxicants thinking that they will make us happy, but only when our minds are clear does happiness truly become available to us.

We should also be diligent in doing good deeds. If there's any work that can bring happiness to ourselves or to others, we should do it without hesitation. Even when work benefits others, we too taste the fruit of happiness from it. These good deeds are blessings, and the happiness that comes from doing them will surely follow.

*"To be humble and polite in manner,*
*To be grateful and content with a simple life,*
*Not missing the occasion to learn the Dharma—*
*This is the greatest happiness."*

To be humble means that you don't put yourself above somebody else. We can learn to be humble and to have reverence for all others, even when they are younger than we are. A young child deserves to be treated with humility and respect.

Young children often invoke a true sense of contentment and gratitude, for they are content with very little. A stick can provide hours of joy and entertainment to a child. In order to be happy, we have to learn to live simply. When we live simply, we have much more time and we can be in touch with the many wonders of life. Living simply is the criterion for the new culture, the new civilization. With the development of technology, people lead more and more complicated lives. Shopping has replaced other activities as our mode for satisfying ourselves. The criterion for being happy is to live simply and to have harmony and peace in yourself and between yourself and the people around you, without aggressiveness, irritation, and anger. We must know the limit, we must know how much is enough. This is the antidote for wanting more and more and more. You know what is sufficient, what is enough for you.

There is a Vietnamese proverb, "Tri tuc, tien tuc, dai tuc, ha thoi tuc." That means, settling for "good enough" is enough. If we wait until all our needs and wants are met, we may wait forever. "Tri tuc" means "good enough." "Good enough" means being content with the minimum amount necessary. Your shirt and pair of shoes can last another year. It's all right for three or four people to share a desk for studying, there's no need for each to have her own desk. Settling for "good enough" in terms of simple living will bring us contentment, satisfaction, and happiness immediately. As long as we think our lives are not good enough, we will not have happiness. As soon as we realize our lives are good enough, happiness immediately appears. That is the practice of contentment.

In Vietnam there's a school of Buddhism called the Four Gratitudes. Just by practicing gratitude, we can find happiness. We must be grateful to our ancestors, our parents, our teachers, our friends, the Earth, the sky, the trees, the grass, the animals, the soil, the stones. Looking at the sunlight or at the forest, we feel gratitude. Looking at our breakfast, we feel gratitude. When we live in the spirit of gratitude, there will be much happiness in our life. The one who is grateful is the one who has much happiness, while the one who is ungrateful will not be able to have happiness.

If someone offers you a teaching, a Dharma talk, take it. Seize any opportunity to learn the Dharma. A Dharma talk is not a lecture, but an opportunity to open ourselves up and allow the deepest levels of our consciousness to be penetrated and nourished by the Dharma. Listening to a Dharma talk can take the misunderstanding and ignorance out of us. It can take away our craving, anger, and hatred. The more toxins we remove, the more our hearts will feel light and free, and happiness will be possible. Happiness grows from inside out.

Those who conduct their life according to this principle will have lasting happiness.

*"To persevere and be open to change,*
*To have regular contact with monks and nuns,*
*And to fully participate in Dharma discussions—*
*This is the greatest happiness."*

When we can yield to reason and let someone correct us without becoming angry or resentful, then we will find that happiness remains with us. It is incredibly difficult, but when our brothers and our sisters point out our faults, the best thing we can do is put our palms together and bow in appreciation, with graciousness on our faces and in our hearts.

The benefit in being close to a monk or nun is the opportunity to learn the Dharma. That is why young men and women like to hang around monks and nuns at the temple. This is a very great blessing!

A Dharma discussion is an opportunity to express ourselves and to listen and learn from others. We can share our joys, difficulties, insights, experiences, and questions. Using loving speech and deep listening, we can also focus on important matters of concern, such as how to create a good environment for our children, our children's children, our larger community, and the Earth as a whole.

*"To live diligently and attentively,*
*To perceive the Noble Truths,*
*And to realize nirvana—*
*This is the greatest happiness."*

To live diligently and attentively means walking, standing, lying down, sitting, working, eating and doing everything in mindfulness.

The Four Noble Truths are at the heart of Buddhist practice.[16] Thanks to the Four Noble Truths, we will be able to practice and realize nirvana. Nirvana is something very concrete, the absence of afflictions and the presence of solidity, freedom, and well-being. To realize nirvana is to be completely liberated and cease all suffering while we are living in the world. All afflictions are dissolved, and only perfect equanimity remains. This is the full definition of happiness.

Because we've planted good seeds in the past, we now have the opportunity to live among the sages. In a good environment it's easy for us to plant good seeds—seeds of peace, joy, community, and happiness. Today we are blessed to be able to sit in the middle of a healthy Sangha that practices with diligence and with ease; we are reaping the benefit of the good seeds we have planted in the past. We need to continue our path and not abandon our good environment.

*"To live in the world*
*With your heart undisturbed by the world,*
*With all sorrows ended, dwelling in peace—*
*This is the greatest happiness."*

Although we are still living in this mundane world, our minds can be imperturbable. We don't need to be flustered by all that we see and hear. The practice of letting go is essential for our happiness. We distance ourselves from the influences that destroy our body and mind, so that we are able to release the many worries and concerns that consume us and prevent us from getting in touch with the wonders of life that we need for our nourishment. There are many things we cannot let go of, and so we miss the opportunity to get in touch with what is more important, and with what is refreshing and healing that is always available to us. We get caught in a kind of prison. Recognizing that these worries and concerns are not really important, we are able to release them, and suddenly happiness comes right away.

It's like when you leave the city behind to go to the countryside. It may take forty-five minutes or an hour to get out of the city, and when the hills begin to appear and the breeze begins to caress your face, you feel so happy because you've been able to leave the city behind you. All of us have had this kind of experience.

Have you ever met someone who seems to be skilled in the art of letting go? A friend or a teacher can remind us and help us let go of worry, craving, and concern, so we can be free to encounter the wonders of life that are in the here and the now. If we see someone living in this world who is not disturbed by the ebb and flow of life, not enmeshed in afflictions, that person has freedom, that person is solid. To see such a person is the highest blessing. When we master this quality, all of our worldly afflictions dissolve and we become indestructible, completely at peace. We can become that person by practicing happiness in the present moment.

*"For the one who accomplishes this*
*Is unvanquished wherever she goes;*
*Always he is safe and happy—*
*Happiness lives within oneself."*

The World-Honored One has said that we should not predict the future based on what happened in the past. We need to base the future on our own actions in the present. Our actions are our karma, and so are our thoughts, our speech, our intentions, and our attitude. If we live in the Dharma, we can generate our own blessings. Our happiness is a lasting one that can be carried on to the next life. We can find happiness no matter what situation we might be thrown into.

Wherever we may go, we will feel the secure protection of the Dharma. Wherever we may go, we will feel strong and solid. The solidity comes from the practice. The greatest blessing is not the one that falls down from the sky and is handed to us. The greatest blessing is the happiness that each of us can generate for ourselves.

*notes*

1. This sutra was translated from Pali to Chinese by the Parthian monk, An Shih Kao at the Lo Yang Center in China during the later Han dynasty (140–171 C.E.). The ancient form of this sutra is the culmination of several smaller works combined. The sutra is entirely in accord with both the Mahayana and Theravada traditions of Buddhism.

2. The four elements are earth, air, water, and fire.

3. The five skandhas are forms, feelings, perceptions, mental formations, and consciousness.

4. A bodhisattva, "awakening being," is someone committed to enlightening oneself and others so that all may be liberated from suffering.

5. The four kinds of Mara are unwholesome mental factors, five skandhas, death, and distractions (e.g., fantasies or forgetfulness).

6. The three worlds are desire and passion, form (without desire and passion), and formlessness (only mental functioning).

7. The five desires are being wealthy, being beautiful, being ambitious, finding pleasure in eating, and being lazy.

8. Dharmakaya means the body of the teaching of awakening.

9. Nirvana is liberation from birth and death.

10. The Four Noble Truths are suffering, the cause of suffering, the end of suffering, and the Eightfold Path.

**11.** Dependent origination (Sanskrit, *pratitya samutpada*) means that any phenomenon arises and exists not on its own, but in a mutually interdependent web of cause and effect with all other phenomena.

**12.** See Endnote 7.

**13.** The Four Foundations of Mindfulness are body, feeling, state of mind, and mental contents.

**14.** The Mangala Sutta, sometimes called the Mahamangala Sutta, appears in the Sutta-Nipata and in the Khuddakapatha. It also appears in the Jataka (tales of the Buddha's earlier births, often in animal-fable form).

**15.** For the Beginning Anew Ceremony, see Thich Nhat Hanh, *Chanting from the Heart* (Berkeley, CA: Parallax Press, 2006). [Formerly *The Plum Village Chanting and Recitation Book* (Parallax Press, 2000).]

**16.** See Endnote 10.

Individuals, couples, and families are invited to
practice the art of mindful living in the tradition of
Thich Nhat Hanh at retreat communities in France
and the United States. For information, please visit
www.plumvillage.org or contact:

Plum Village
13 Martineau
33580 Dieulivol, France
info@plumvillage.org

Green Mountain Dharma Center
P.O. Box 182
Hartland Four Corners, VT 05049
mfmaster@vermontel.net
Tel: (802) 436-1103

Deer Park Monastery
2499 Melru Lane
Escondido, CA 92026
deerpark@plumvillage.org
Tel: (760) 291-1003

For a worldwide directory of Sanghas practicing
in the tradition of Thich Nhat Hanh, please visit
www.iamhome.org.

**Parallax Press,** a nonprofit organization, publishes books on engaged Buddhism and the practice of mindfulness by Thich Nhat Hanh and other authors. All of Thich Nhat Hanh's work is available at our online store and in our free catalog. For a copy of the catalog, please contact:

Parallax Press
www.parallax.org
P.O. Box 7355
Berkeley, CA 94707
Tel: (510) 525-0101